# ABC's OF SICKLE CELL DISEASE

*ABC's of Sickle Cell Disease*

By Elle Cole

Published by CleverlyChanging

Cover Design: by Kate Hamernik

Illustrations: Kate Hamernik

Layout & Design: David Cavins

For information about special discounts available for bulk purchases, sales promotions, fund-raising and educational needs contact: Contact@CleverlyChanging.com or call 410-429-7043.

ISBN: 978-1-7350498-9-2 hardback

ISBN: 978-1-7350498-4-7 paperback

ISBN: 978-1-7350498-3-0 eBook

Printed in the United States of America.

# ABC's oF Sickle Cell Disease

This book is dedicated to the most amazing Sickle Cell Warrior I know, Laila. I want you to know that Mommy, Daddy, and Maya love you!

This book will help explain Sickle Cell Disease to children. Please consult a physician for specific treatments and diagnoses.

Each year, about 1 in 13 African American babies are born with Sickle Cell Trait. Also, 1 in 365 African American children are born with Sickle Cell Disease. About 1 out of every 16,300 Hispanic-American children will be born with Sickle Cell Disease (CDC.gov).

# The Letter A is For Anemia

Doctors take care of their patients (people who are ill) who do not make enough blood; this condition is called anemia. Anemia occurs when a person's body has a lower number of red blood cells. These red blood cells are supposed to carry oxygen throughout their entire body. Anemia can make you feel tired like you don't want to move. When people who have Sickle Cell Disease feel sleepy, they should take a nap.

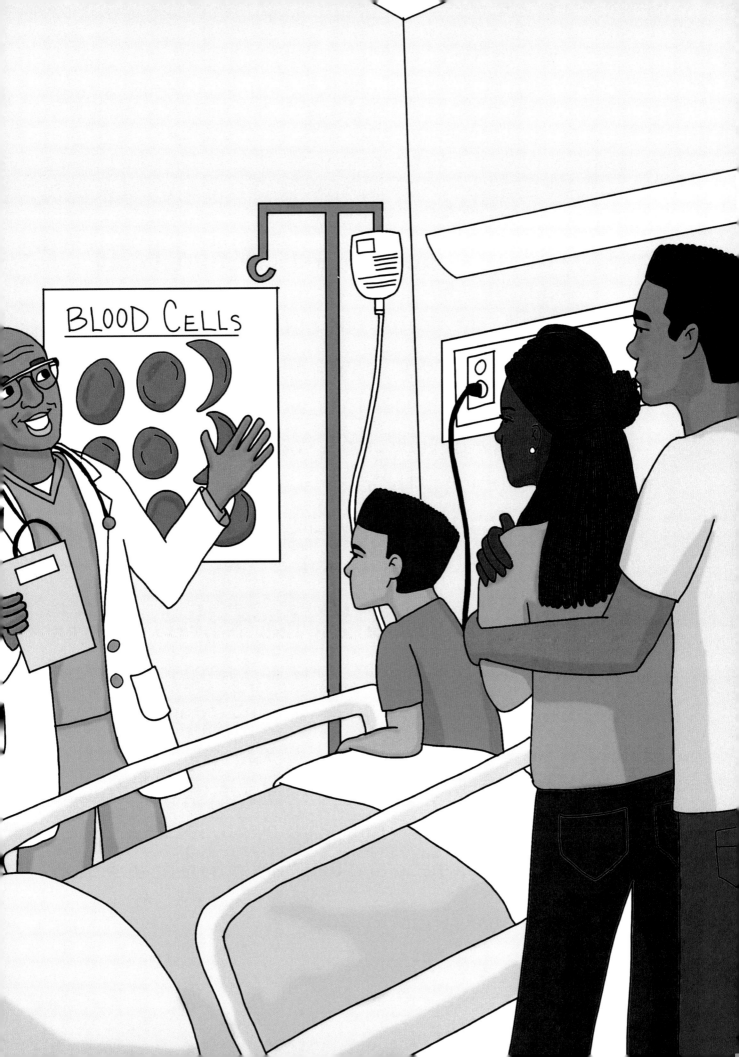

# The Letter B is For Blood Cells

When you go to the doctor, one of the doctor's helpers—called a nurse—will need to take a look at your blood. You will need to sit still in your chair while the nurse uses special tools to get some of your blood. You may feel a pinch, but it won't hurt for long. The nurse will put the needle in your skin to fill small bottles with your blood so that the doctor can have a closer look at how your body is working for you.

One of the tools that doctors and their helpers use to get your blood is called a needle. You don't have to be afraid of the needle; the doctors' helpers are not trying to hurt you. They want to help you by collecting your blood. Sometimes, it can help to play music to ease your mind and distract you while the nurse fills each tube with blood. It can also be helpful to turn your head and look in a different direction.

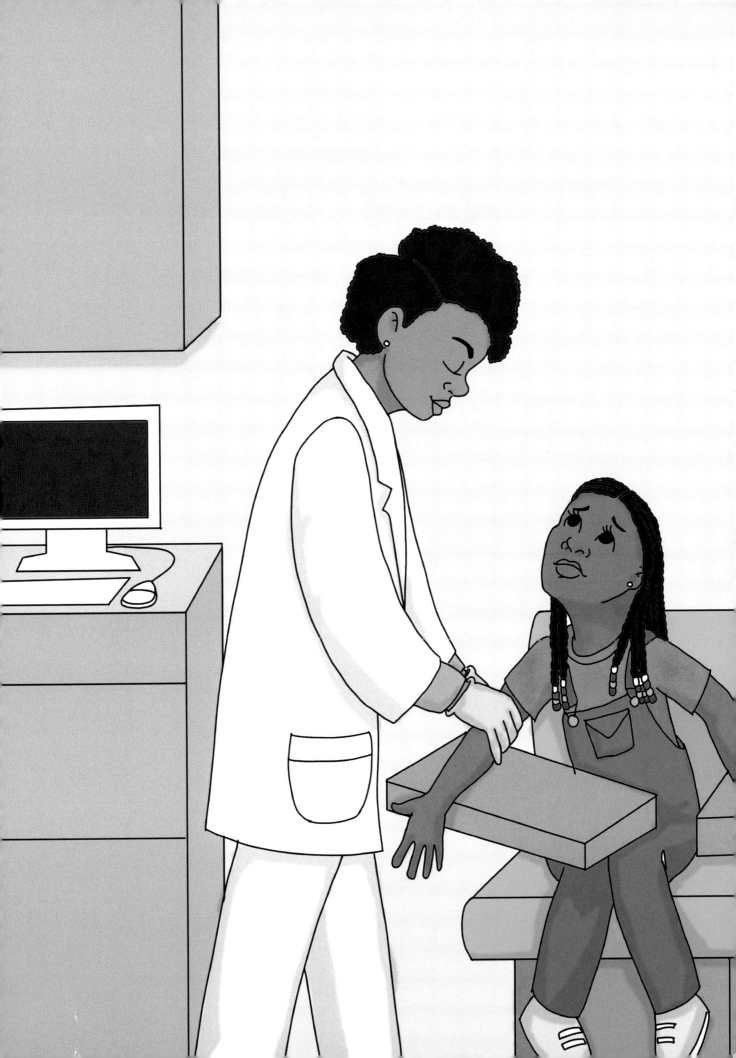

# C

## The Letter C is For Cells

Cells are in every living thing like people, plants, and animals. There are three types of blood cells in your body: white blood cells, red blood cells, and platelets—the blood cells in your body float inside your blood vessels. Your white blood cells help you fight off germs, and your red blood cells help your body by carrying the oxygen it needs. Platelets, the smallest blood cells, help your blood clot (or clump together to become a solid mass like when you get a scab).

# The Letter D is For Disorder

Sickle Cell Disease is a blood disorder. The disorder affects your body and can cause you to get sick. When you are sick, you may feel uncomfortable and hurt in different places on your body. Sometimes, the pain will only be in one place and, at other times, you can ache all over.

There are different types of Sickle Cell Disorders. Some are called Sickle Cell Anemia, Sickle Cell-C Disease, Sickle Cell-E Disease, and Sickle Cell-S-Beta-Thalassemia.

# The Letter E is For Exercise

Exercising is good for everybody's body, but it is important to tell someone if you feel too hot, cold, or tired while you are exercising. Listen to your body, and when your body tells you that you are tired, you should stop and rest. If your body tells you that you are too cold, you need to warm up with a blanket. If you are too hot, you need to drink water and let your body cool down.

# The Letter F is For Fatigue

Sometimes you will feel tired or fatigued. If your body feels sleepy, sit still, be quiet, and take a break. You may want to sleep a lot, and you may not have enough energy to play and do other things you enjoy. Anemia and some medications can cause sickle cell patients to feel fatigued.

It is essential to have a regular sleep schedule to help refresh your body every day. Sleep can help your body as you grow. It can help keep you healthy, focus better, and have more energy when you want to play.

# The Letter G is For Genetics

Sickle Cell Disease is a genetic disorder, which means you get it from your parents through messengers called genes. Genes are a set of instructions a person receives from both parents before a person is born. We call the body's instruction manual DNA because these messengers tell a person's body what to do. All patients who have the disease inherited it, which means they were born with it, and other people cannot catch Sickle Cell Disease.

# The Letter H is For Hematologist

A hematologist is a special blood doctor who went to school to learn how to help people with blood disorders like Sickle Cell Disease. Your blood doctor wants to help you feel better, so it is good to tell the doctor how you feel and ask questions when you don't understand what you may be feeling or what he or she is explaining.

# The Letter I is For Inherited

Children inherit or receive different qualities from their mom and dad. For example, children receive their hair and eye colors from their parents. You received other traits from your mom and dad that make you into the person you are. For example, your eyes may look like your dad's eyes. Sometimes people can inherit genes that do not work correctly in their bodies.

# The Letter J is For Jaundice

When the white part of your eyes and your skin look yellow, doctors call it jaundice. Sometimes, your eyes might look yellow because your body is working very hard to make new blood cells for you to use. And sometimes, when your blood is fighting hard to give your body what it needs, the white part of your eyes turns yellow. Yellow jaundice occurs because red blood cells break down too fast.

# The Letter K is For Knowledge

Doctors are still learning more to help cure Sickle Cell Disease for people all over the world. As you grow, we will continue to learn more about it as well. So we can keep you as healthy as possible. All of the information and research gathered by doctors and other healthcare professionals help us understand the disorder better.

# The Letter L is For Love

Your family loves you very much. Even when you are sick and not feeling well, your family's love for you will never change. You are loved no matter what happens. Remember that love listens, love supports, and love hopes for the best.

# The Letter M is For Medicine

Many kids who have Sickle Cell Disease need to take medicine to stay healthy. When some children are young, doctors may ask their parents to give them penicillin twice a day to help them stay healthy. There are other medicines that doctors may prescribe, and it is helpful to set reminders so you and your parents can remember to take your medication at the right time each day.

# The Letter N is For Newborn Screening

When babies are born, doctors give them a blood test. The doctor checks a small amount of babies' blood to see if they have Sickle Cell Disease. Children who have Sickle Cell Disease are encouraged to start visiting a Hematologist for treatment.

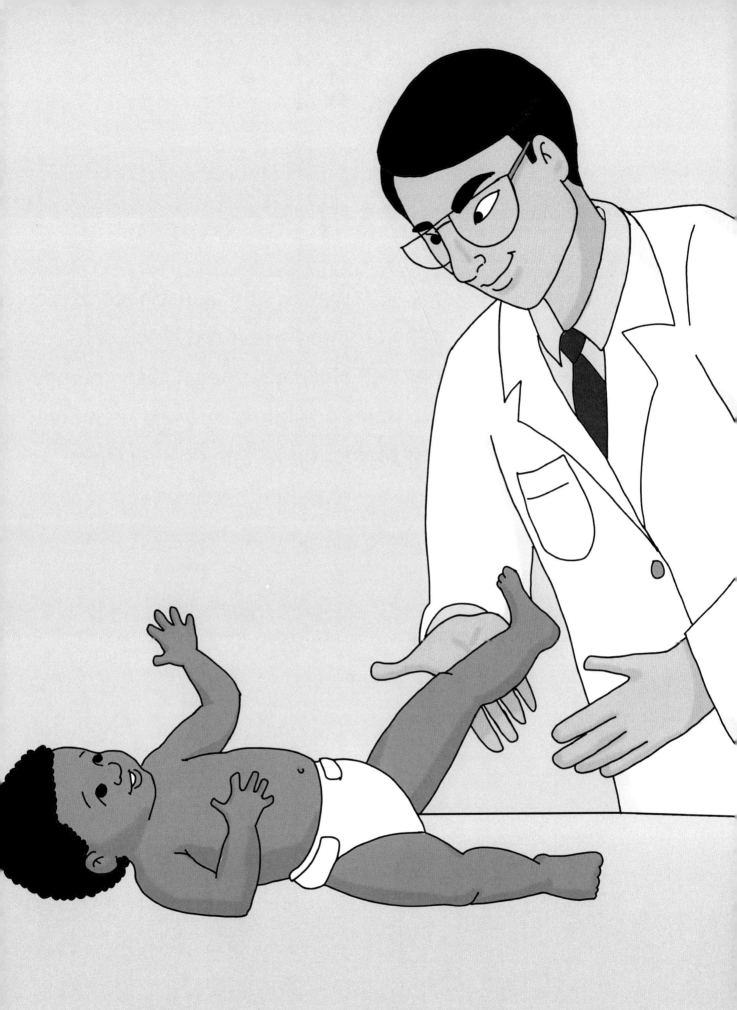

# The Letter O is For Oxygen

All living things like people, animals, and plants need oxygen to live. Hemoglobin is the protein in your red blood cells that carries oxygen. Your red blood cells begin their journey from your bone marrow, travel to your heart, and then are pumped into other areas of your body. One of their main goals is to give your body the oxygen it needs so you can survive.

Red Blood Cell

Sickled Red Blood Cells

# The Letter P is For Pain Crisis

Sometimes, people with Sickle Cell Disease will feel a lot of pain in their bodies. When the pain causes a person to hurt badly, it is called a crisis and can last several hours or several days. The pain comes from red blood cells that get stuck in your blood vessels and cannot supply the oxygen you need.

# The Letter Q is For Questions

There is so much information for people to learn about Sickle Cell Disease. Remember, you can always ask a doctor, nurse, or family member if you have questions about Sickle Cell Disease or the human body. Sometimes, you or your parents can write down your questions that come to mind to ask the doctor at your next appointment.

# The Letter R is For Remember

Remember that it is vital to take care of yourself even when you don't want to. If you are not feeling well when you are away from your parents, tell an adult so you can get help. People living with Sickle Cell Disease can have challenges, but with love, care, and following the doctor's orders, they can lead a healthy, inspiring life.

# The Letter S is For Sickle

Doctors call blood cells sickled when they are not shaped like circles but like the letter c or shaped like a banana. Sometimes, when your blood is sickled, it can get stuck in your body and block your blood vessels, which hurts.

**What is Sickle Cell Disease?** Sickle Cell Disease occurs when most or all of the red blood cells in a person's body are sickled.

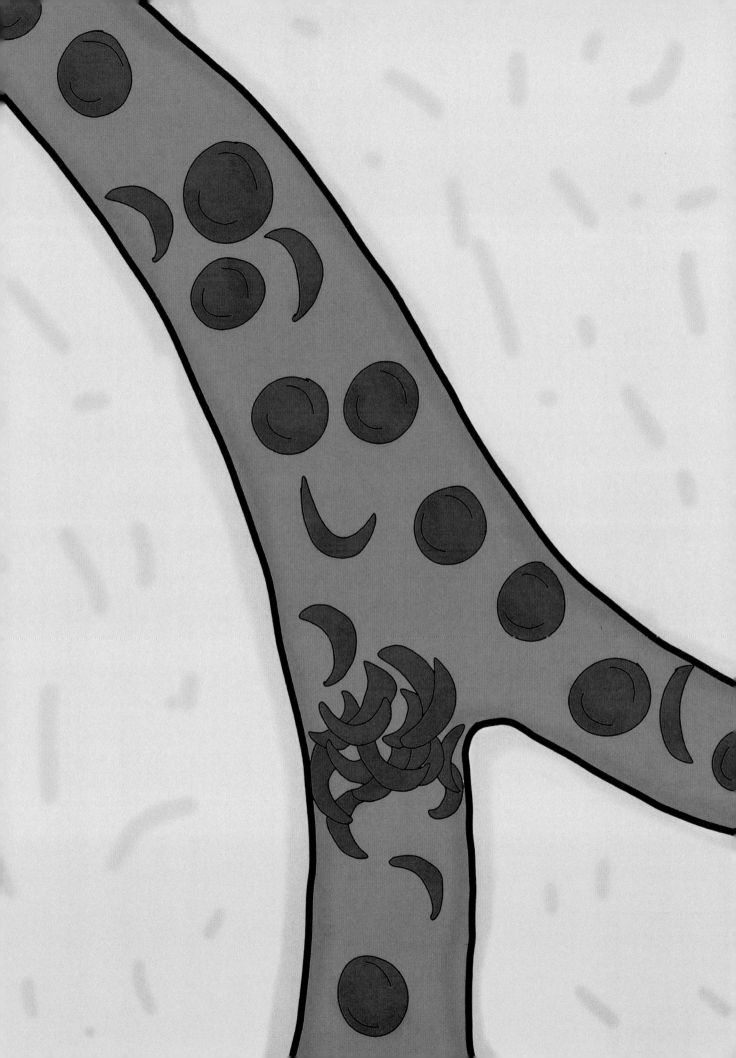

# The Letter T is For Transcranial Doppler Test (TCD)

Once a year, some children with Sickle Cell Disease take a TCD test. A TCD test is the same as a stroke screen risk test. Stroke screening measures a child's risk for having a stroke. The test will tell your doctor how the blood is flowing within your arteries. When you were in your mom's stomach, the doctors used a similar machine to look at you.

# The Letter U is For Ultrasound

Doctor's helpers use an ultrasound machine to take pictures of different parts of the inside of your body. This machine is not painful, but it may tickle. It is also the same machine used when you take a stroke screen test. During the TCD, if you are quiet and listen closely, you can hear the sound of your blood pumping inside your brain.

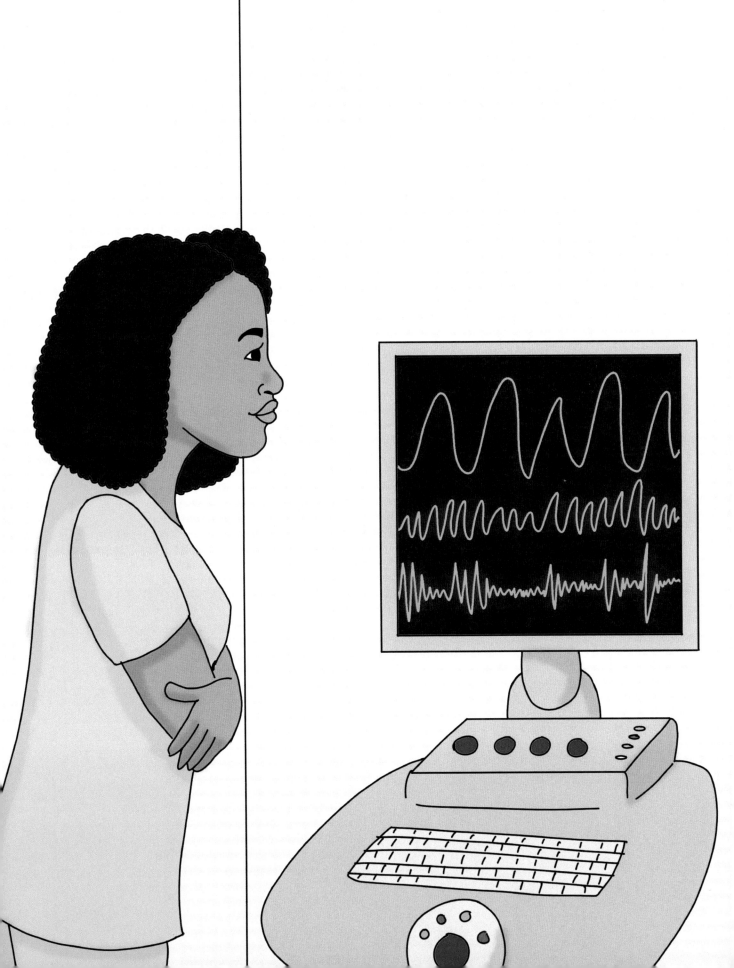

# The Letter V is For Vegetables

You need to eat healthy foods that have a lot of fiber. This food is beneficial for your body because it gives it the proper nutrients to produce strong red blood cells. Some of these foods are nuts, lima beans, carrots, cabbage, spinach, and broccoli. It is essential to eat a regular balanced diet. There are five main food groups that you should eat from:

1. Vegetables
2. Fruits
3. Grains
4. Proteins
5. Dairy foods

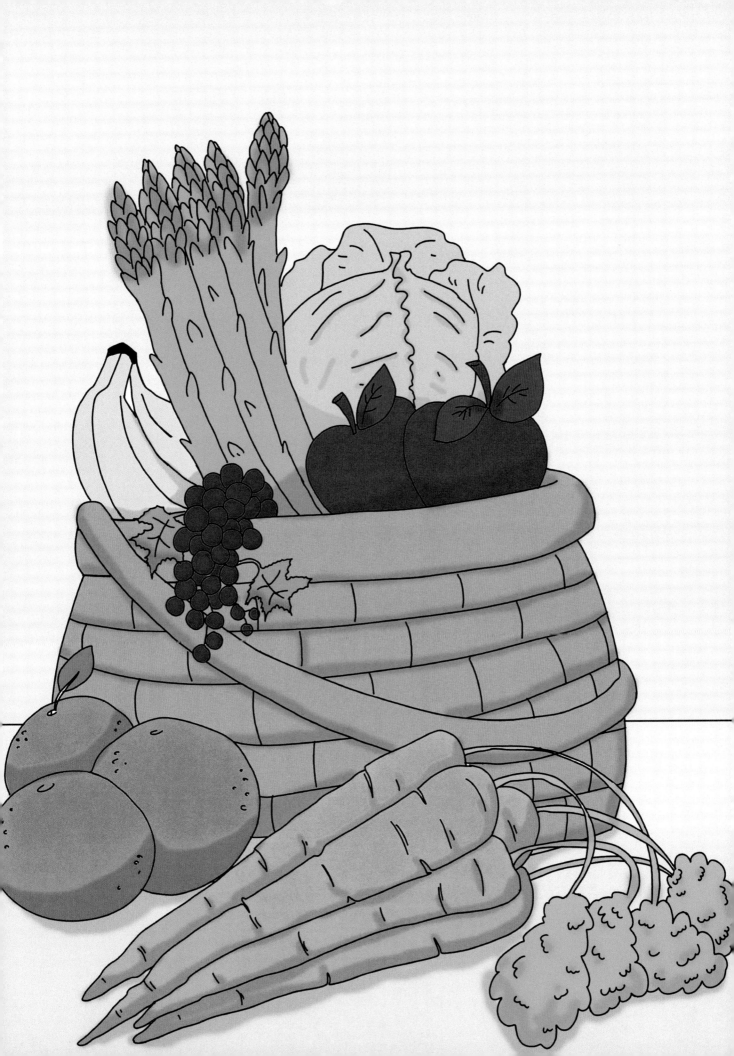

# The Letter W is For Water

Your body needs lots and lots and lots of water, so drink water every day throughout the day. When a person doesn't get enough water in their body, it is called dehydration. Water can also help push your body's blood cells through your blood vessels better.

# The Letter x is For x-ray

Sometimes, doctors may want to see your bones and joints' pictures to see how you are growing. They may also take photos to see if there is swelling that might occur during a crisis or to know if you have an infection in your lungs called pneumonia. The machine that takes the pictures does not hurt, but you will need to sit or stand still so the image will be clear.

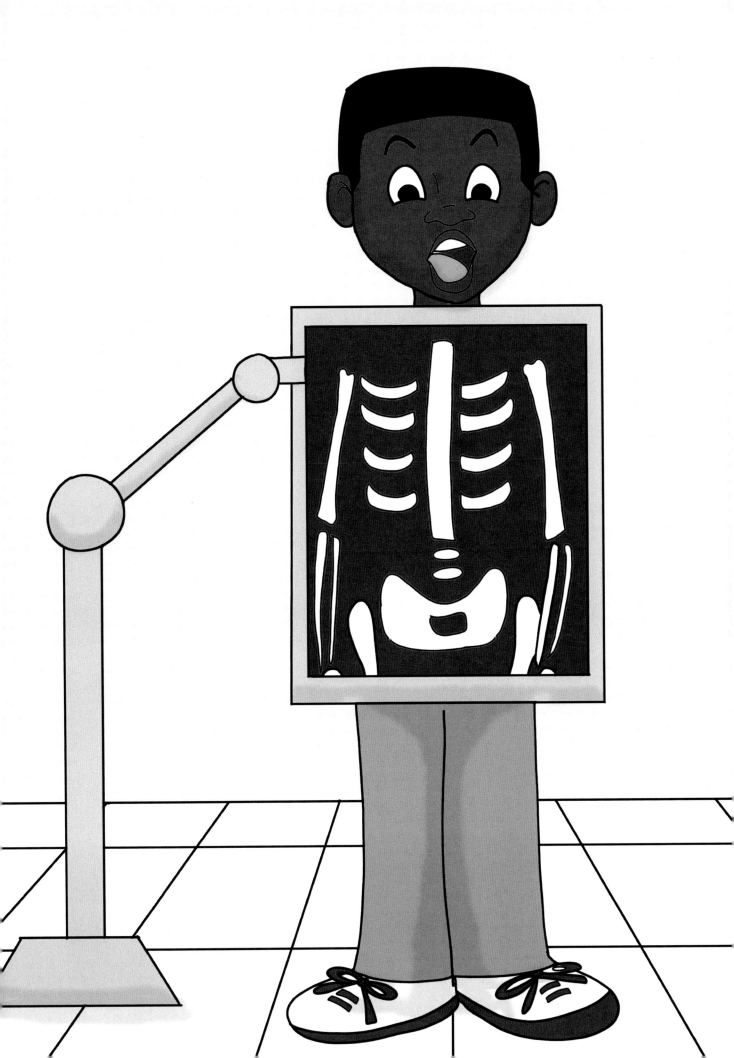

# The Letter Y is For Years

You may have Sickle Cell Disease throughout your life. Therefore, have a plan to establish healthy habits every day. By eating healthy, drinking plenty of water, washing your hands regularly, visiting your doctor, taking the medicine your doctor gives you and getting enough rest, you will be able to enjoy your life for years to come.

# Z

## The Letter Z is For Zero

Our goal is that one day, there will be zero pain for people with sickled blood cells. We hope that people living with Sickle Cell Disease will be able to live healthy, pain-free lives.

People who live with Sickle Cell Disease can achieve success and have different types of careers. They can become doctors, nurses, attorneys, artists, preachers, teachers, therapists, authors, models, actors, dancers, and more. Don't let Sickle Cell Disease stop you from living your dreams.

# About the Author

Elle Cole is a mom of twin daughters, one of whom is living with Sickle Cell Disease. After she and her husband learned that their daughter had Sickle Cell Disease, she wished there was a guide to help parents and kids understand more about the disease. She wrote: *ABC's of Sickle Cell Disease* to help her daughter learn more about living with Sickle Cell Disease.

She serves as a parent advocate for Sickle Cell Disease and Type 1 Diabetes. She is an ambassador for St. Jude Children's Research Hospital. She also raises awareness about genetic disorders and autoimmune diseases to help improve the quality of life for people living with these illnesses.

Elle is a recipient of a Bronze Congressional Award and has been featured on NPR, ABC 7, BBC World Service Radio, NBC Washington, and a guest on many podcasts. She is a writer, motivational speaker, podcast host, and social media strategist.

She is also a passionate storyteller and podcast host. You can listen to The Cleverly Changing Homeschool Podcast on Apple podcast or her parenting blog CleverlyChanging.com.

**Did you find this book interesting or helpful?** If so, please leave a review on Amazon, request this book at your local library, and ask a doctor to share it with other patients.

Made in the USA
Middletown, DE
17 October 2023

40329969R00033